A FIRST LATIN-AMERICAN FLUTE ALBUM

EDITED BY TREVOR WYE

for flute and piano

NOVELLO PUBLISHING LIMITED

Order No: NOV120634

CONTENTS

PREFACE

A fascination of many years standing for the rhythms and melodies of South American music has resulted in the compiling of these volumes. The rhythms, for those of us from other countries are, at first, difficult but with a little practice, they will become easier. Those pieces in five beats in a bar are best practised at one beat in a bar. Where marked 8va, this is optional, though Latin-American flautists are noted for their ease in the top register.

Ornaments have been suggested; more can be added. A bass + percussion part can be added, if required. Syncopation, in this music, is impossible to write down accurately. The solution is to relax and enjoy this special rhythmic style.

I am indebted to Robert Scott for his immense patience in arranging the piano parts.

Trevor Wye

The separate flute part is inserted

A FIRST LATIN-AMERICAN FLUTE ALBUM

Edited by Trevor Wye

1. ESTILO
(Style)

Folk

2. MARACAIBO EN LA NOCHE

(Maracaibo at Night)

A. Molero

3. MILONGA

Angel Lasala

4. URPILA

Folk Tune
adapted by **Gustavo Samela**

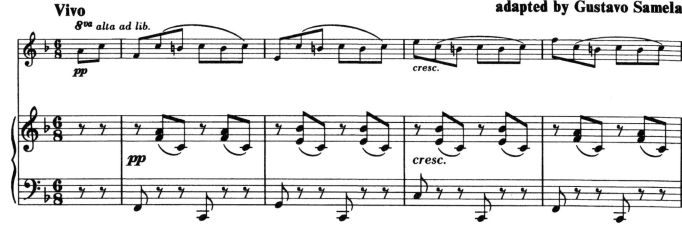

6

5. EL DIABLO SUELTO!

(The Devil–may–care!)

H. Hernandez

6. EL CONTRABANDO
(Smuggling)

Folk

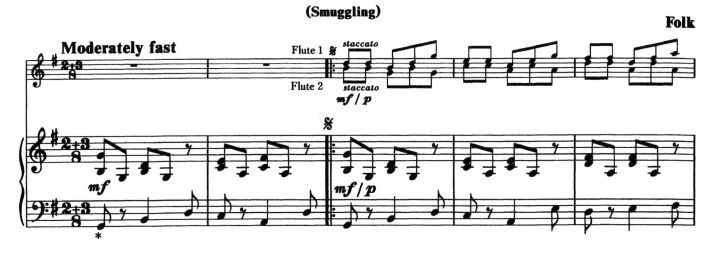

* Percussion rhythm | ♪ ♩ ♪ | or | ♫ ♩ ♪ | optional

7. JUNANA

Folk

8. LA PARTIDA

(The Departure)

C. Bonet

9. CIELITO
(Darling)

Angel Lasala

10. CAMINO PELAO
(Road to Pelao)

Folk

MUSIC FOR FLUTE

TUTORS

WYE, Trevor
A BEGINNER'S BOOK FOR THE FLUTE
A PRACTICE BOOK FOR THE FLUTE:
VOLUME 1 Tone (Cassette also available)
VOLUME 2 Technique
VOLUME 3 Articulation
VOLUME 4 Intonation and vibrato
VOLUME 5 Breathing and scales
VOLUME 6 Advanced Practice
PROPER FLUTE PLAYING

SOLO

ALBUM
ed Trevor Wye
MUSIC FOR SOLO FLUTE
This attractive collection draws together under
one cover 11 major works representing the
fundamental solo flute repertoire, edited in a
clear and practical form.

trans Gordon Saunders
EIGHT TRADITIONAL JAPANESE PIECES
Gordon Saunders has selected and transcribed
these pieces for tenor recorder solo or flute from
the traditional folk music of Japan.

FLUTE AND PIANO

ALBUMS
arr Barrie Carson Turner
CHRISTMAS FUN BOOK
CLASSICAL POPS FUN BOOK
ITALIAN OPERA FUN BOOK
MOZART FUN BOOK
POP CANTATA FUN BOOK
POPULAR CLASSICS FUN BOOK
RAGTIME FUN BOOK
TV THEME FUN BOOK

arr Trevor Wye
A VERY EASY BAROQUE ALBUM, Vols. 1 & 2
A VERY EASY CLASSICAL ALBUM
A VERY EASY ROMANTIC ALBUM
A VERY EASY 20TH CENTURY ALBUM
A FIRST LATIN-AMERICAN FLUTE ALBUM
A SECOND LATIN-AMERICAN FLUTE ALBUM

BENNETT, Richard Rodney
SUMMER MUSIC

COUPERIN, François
arr Trevor Wye
A COUPERIN ALBUM

ELGAR, Edward
arr Trevor Wye
AN ELGAR FLUTE ALBUM

FRASER, Shena
SONATINA

GALWAY, James
THE MAGIC FLUTE OF JAMES GALWAY
SHOWPIECES

HARRIS, Paul
CLOWNS

HURD, Michael
SONATINA

McCABE, John
PORTRAITS

RAMEAU, Jean Philippe
arr Trevor Wye
A RAMEAU ALBUM

REEMAN, John
SIX FOR ONE

SATIE, Erik
arr Trevor Wye
A SATIE FLUTE ALBUM

SCHUBERT, Franz
arr Trevor Wye
THEME AND VARIATIONS D.935 No.3

SCHURMANN, Gerard
SONATINA

VIVALDI, Antonio
arr Trevor Wye
A VIVALDI ALBUM

NOVELLO PUBLISHING LIMITED

Order No: NOV120634

A FIRST LATIN-AMERICAN FLUTE ALBUM
Edited by Trevor Wye

1. ESTILO
(Style)

FLUTE

Folk

2. MARACAIBO EN LA NOCHE
(Maracaibo at night)

A. Molero

FLUTE
3. MILONGA

Angel Lasala

4. URPILA

Folk Tune
adapted by Gustavo Samela

D.C. tutto

5. EL DIABLO SUELTO!

(The Devil-man-care!)

H. Hernandez

6. EL CONTRABANDO

(Smuggling)

Folk

FLUTE

FLUTE

7. JUNANA

Folk

Allegro ♩.+♩=66
(*8va alta ad lib.*)

FLUTE
8. LA PARTIDA
(The Departure)

C. Bonet

9. CIELITO
(Darling)

Angel Lasala

10. CAMINO PELAO
(Road to Pelao)

Folk

MUSIC FOR FLUTE

TUTORS

WYE, Trevor
A BEGINNER'S BOOK FOR THE FLUTE
A PRACTICE BOOK FOR THE FLUTE:
VOLUME 1 Tone (Cassette also available)
VOLUME 2 Technique
VOLUME 3 Articulation
VOLUME 4 Intonation and vibrato
VOLUME 5 Breathing and scales
VOLUME 6 Advanced Practice
PROPER FLUTE PLAYING

SOLO

ALBUM
ed Trevor Wye
MUSIC FOR SOLO FLUTE
This attractive collection draws together under
one cover 11 major works representing the
fundamental solo flute repertoire, edited in a
clear and practical form.

trans Gordon Saunders
EIGHT TRADITIONAL JAPANESE PIECES
Gordon Saunders has selected and transcribed
these pieces for tenor recorder solo or flute from
the traditional folk music of Japan.

FLUTE AND PIANO

ALBUMS
arr Barrie Carson Turner
CHRISTMAS FUN BOOK
CLASSICAL POPS FUN BOOK
ITALIAN OPERA FUN BOOK
MOZART FUN BOOK
POP CANTATA FUN BOOK
POPULAR CLASSICS FUN BOOK
RAGTIME FUN BOOK
TV THEME FUN BOOK

arr Trevor Wye
A VERY EASY BAROQUE ALBUM, Vols. 1 & 2
A VERY EASY CLASSICAL ALBUM
A VERY EASY ROMANTIC ALBUM
A VERY EASY 20TH CENTURY ALBUM
A FIRST LATIN-AMERICAN FLUTE ALBUM
A SECOND LATIN-AMERICAN FLUTE ALBUM

BENNETT, Richard Rodney
SUMMER MUSIC

COUPERIN, François
arr Trevor Wye
A COUPERIN ALBUM

ELGAR, Edward
arr Trevor Wye
AN ELGAR FLUTE ALBUM

FRASER, Shena
SONATINA

GALWAY, James
THE MAGIC FLUTE OF JAMES GALWAY
SHOWPIECES

HARRIS, Paul
CLOWNS

HURD, Michael
SONATINA

McCABE, John
PORTRAITS

RAMEAU, Jean Philippe
arr Trevor Wye
A RAMEAU ALBUM

REEMAN, John
SIX FOR ONE

SATIE, Erik
arr Trevor Wye
A SATIE FLUTE ALBUM

SCHUBERT, Franz
arr Trevor Wye
THEME AND VARIATIONS D.935 No.3

SCHURMANN, Gerard
SONATINA

VIVALDI, Antonio
arr Trevor Wye
A VIVALDI ALBUM

NOVELLO PUBLISHING LIMITED
14/15 Berners Street, London W1T 3LJ

Order No: NOV120634